Contents

Pathfinder 24

A CILT series for language teachers

Exploring otherness
- an approach to cultural awareness

Barry Jones

Other titles in the PATHFINDER series:

Reading for pleasure in a foreign language (Ann Swarbrick)
Communication re-activated: teaching pupils with learning difficulties
    (Bernardette Holmes)
Yes - but will they behave? Managing the interactive classroom
    (Susan Halliwell)
On target - teaching in the target language (Susan Halliwell and Barry Jones)
Bridging the gap: GCSE to 'A' level (John Thorogood and Lid King)
Making the case for languages (Alan Moys and Richard Townsend)
Languages home and away (Alison Taylor)
Being creative (Barry Jones)
Departmental planning and schemes of work (Clive Hurren)
Progressing through the Attainment Targets (Ian Lane)
Continuous assessment and recording (John Thorogood)
Fair enough? Equal opportunities and modern languages (Vee Harris)
Improve your image: the effective use of the OHP
    (Daniel Tierney and Fay Humphreys)
Not bothered? Motivating reluctant learners in Key Stage 4
    (Jenifer Alison)
Grammar matters (Susan Halliwell)
Differentiation (Anne Convery and Do Coyle)
Drama in the languages classroom (Judith Hamilton and Anne McLeod)
Nightshift - ideas and strategies for homework
    (David Buckland and Mike Short)
Creative use of texts (Bernard Kavanagh and Lynne Upton)
Developing skills for independent reading (Iain Mitchell and Ann Swarbrick)
Keeping on target (Bernardette Holmes)

First published 1995
Copyright © 1995 Centre for Information on Language Teaching and Research
ISBN 1 874016 42 9

Cover by Logos Design
Printed in Great Britain by Oakdale Printing Co Ltd

Published by the Centre for Information on Language Teaching and Research,
20 Bedfordbury, Covent Garden, London WC2N 4LB.

Introduction

'Otherness' is often intriguing. It can be exciting and attractive, as well as bewildering and unsettling. When 'otherness' is experienced at first hand it can prompt all kinds of questions not only about 'others' but also about ourselves and whether we wish to take on or be part of that 'otherness' or not. It can point to differences and similarities which challenge or confirm what we know and feel. It very frequently questions what we believe to be true. For some, 'otherness' is worth exploring, whereas for others contact with it may bring about or even confirm a reluctance to venture into the realms of the unfamiliar and close off not only new worlds but also questions about ourselves. This book seeks to encourage an attitude of openness towards others, and to involve, if possible, the hesitant as well as the enthusiastic.

Within a school setting it is an area of experience which needs careful programming, sensitive handling and an open mind. 'Otherness' is perhaps best described **provisionally.** Learners need to know that further evidence in the form of more experience or new information will always be sought to modify what may appear, at first sight, to be stable features within a culture or way of life. This seems to be a justifiable strategy for, even if 'otherness' remains static for a while, changes may occur within the learner's experience which in turn alter their perceptions of others.

'Awareness' is subject to changes not only in the observed but also in the observer. This book seeks to develop the idea that both 'otherness' and 'awareness' may therefore be relatively provisional. It uses the term 'cultural awareness' with caution because 'culture' is frequently considered by learners to be something to be observed, existing solely as a fixed, stable, self-defining phenomenon. 'Awareness', as used in this book, implies 'knowledge about' as well as 'thinking about' and 'talking about'. In most examples 'awareness' is also seen in terms of ensuing attitudes or evaluative judgements.

The book attempts to outline how opportunities can be created, without leaving the country, for learners to experience, learn about and explore 'otherness', where their role is to define what they interpret this 'otherness' to be. It will suggest strategies which help them to make up their own minds about what 'evidence' of a way of life, set of beliefs, way of behaving means to them. It will encourage them in a practical way to seek more knowledge and more evidence and to be open to the possibility of changes of mind without being unsettled by the experience. It will also offer ways into learner explorations of conventions and modes of behaviour which can enhance communication and without which even relatively casual or brief contact with others may be problematic. It deliberately avoids discussing the merits of travel abroad and activities based on a stay in the other country because this has been extensively covered elsewhere.

1   Study topics

It is believed that an awareness of others can be increased by developing, over time, an understanding of:

- social conventions;
- similarities and differences between groups of different language communities;
- the unfamiliar within a target language community;
- stereotypes as perceived by one linguistic group about another;
- attitudes towards 'others';
- language as culture.

This process can be started by first trying to understand:

- the variety of conventions, attitudes, values, languages in **our** own country or community and more about where and how **we** live.

From these starting points learners will be encouraged to develop an understanding of:

- where and how others live;
- attitudes, values and conventions in other communities.

It is suggested that learners work predominantly from **evidence** and that, as far as possible, teachers encourage an approach which involves discussion and investigation.

EVIDENCE AND DATA

Let us look first at what might constitute the raw material of this approach. Evidence can take many forms. It may be a collection of, say, handwritten self portraits in which teenagers from one language community describe themselves. It may also be the result of enquiries or surveys by questionnaire conducted amongst members of another language community. A beginning list might include such additional items as:

- documents produced by target language speakers, such as timelines, graphs, bar charts, timetables, diagrams;
- interviews;
- textbook extracts;
- objects;
- realia;
- newspaper and magazine articles or information;

- TV programmes;
- video or audio material - the list can be extended by teacher and learner alike.

To gather such materials should be, as far as possible, the responsibility of learners rather than the task of teachers. There are several reasons for this. Firstly, it is time consuming and the involvement of many participants can provide a wide range of evidence which is both desirable and necessary. Secondly, if collected by one person only, the materials would probably reflect that individual's choice and may not therefore be of interest to all. Thirdly, it is always advisable to involve the learners in as much of this work as possible so that they feel part of the process and not just recipients of it. Fourthly, all forms of evidence and data collection make purposeful use of the target language. Learners can write simple letters, compose an occasional FAX, decide on the questions they want to ask in a questionnaire, conduct simple interviews with target language speakers, read and select relevant information; all four language skills can be practised for a real purpose and for a known audience.

There are many opportunities for evidence to be collected. These include:

- oral/written questions to local target language speakers (Foreign Language Assistants, visitors, local community groups...);
- requests for information to be written or provided by local target language speakers (letters, descriptions, notes, realia...);
- class links with target language speakers;
- visits and exchanges during which participants collect not only for themselves but also for those who are not able to participate;
- letters and/or FAX requests to target language organisations at home or abroad.

2 Monitoring and recording developing understandings

To help record developing understandings learners are encouraged to keep a log book of evidence and its interpretation.

In addition, it is strongly recommended also that the teacher has a display board for IMAGES OF US AND OF OTHERS, protected by a sheet of plastic, fixed with double glazing clips, so that the display can be changed easily and regularly, on which learners' views are expressed. The rule here is that views about 'otherness' may be expressed as long as:

- they are supported by hard evidence, also on display
- at some time discussion takes place about the substance of the views expressed
- the IMAGES display board is divided into

PROVISIONAL	PERMANENT

columns so that readers can see which opinions are much less firmly held than others, and which are seeking corroboration or otherwise. It should, however, always be the teacher's intention that **all** views expressed, no matter in which column they are displayed, can be changed in some way when further evidence has been produced and discussion has taken place.

USE OF THE TARGET LANGUAGE

When evaluating evidence the majority of foreign language learners will probably use English. When, however, they are preparing or working from evidence or producing accounts of findings, explanations, descriptions, or working with realia received from another country they can nearly always work in the target language. The implications of this approach are therefore that, where possible, discussion in English takes place in non foreign language lesson time - often schools have considered this topic to be relevant within a Personal and Social Education (PSE) programme - and work in the target language takes place in a foreign languages' lesson. Schools have also developed programmes of work to be done jointly by the Foreign Languages' and the Geography, Humanities, PSE teaching staff.

3   Projects which help promote awareness of others

What follows is a range of projects which can be tried with Year 7 to Year 12. Some are short and last only a lesson or a part of a lesson; others are more extended. For each project an appropriate year group will be suggested (assuming a Year 7 start to foreign language learning), together with a list of materials and a range of learner tasks.

Projects 1 - 9   **Year 7 onwards**
Using 'homemade' evidence

AIM
To make comparisons between aspects of life in the UK and life in the target language country.

MATERIALS
- interview questions and answers and/or
- handwritten personal descriptions about

- likes/dislikes	- pets
- home town	- school life
- weather in home country	- interests and pastimes
- food at home	- opinions about...
- menus for special days	- similarities and differences in home
- family	country / other country
- house	

SOURCE OF MATERIALS
Collected by asking a Foreign Language Assistant (FLA), and/or other native speakers (e.g. in exchange school, partner school, linked class, family) at home or abroad.

POSSIBLE TASKS
Compare evidence from FLA (or others) with similar evidence from UK class and write/say what appeals to the UK pupils. Emphasis here is put on positive opinion and what is attractive rather than what is considered negatively strange or unattractive.

EXAMPLE TASKS
Working from handwritten descriptions:

1. PERSONAL DESCRIPTIONS

- Would you like to meet Patrice? Say why.

Salut!

Je m'appelle Patrice.
Pour me reconnaître:
j'ai une tête amusante. Je porte des lunettes rondes, j'ai des cheveux bruns, un nez rond. Je suis de taille moyenne: 1 mètre soixante-dix. Je suis souvent mal rasé. Je porterai un jean troué, une superbe chemise colorée et des chaussures de clown, taille cinquante-trois.
Je lirai un journal et j'aurai mon parapluie avec moi.

2. DESCRIPTIONS OF THE SEASONS IN A SPECIFIC REGION OF A COUNTRY

- What differences in your daily routine would living in this climate make?

Aux Antilles, il y a deux saisons:

- *le Carême*
- *l'Hivernage*

LES SAISONS

1. *Le Carême*

   Le Carême dure environ 6 mois; de février à juillet. C'est une saison sèche. Elle correspond à la période de 'jeûne' de la religion catholique.

2. *L'Hivernage*

   L'Hivernage dure environ 6 mois: de août à janvier. C'est une saison pluvieuse. C'est aussi la saison des tempêtes tropicales, des ouragans et des cyclones.

- In which part of France might you find this town?
  Say why you think so.

Le temps qu'il fait à

Printemps

*Un peu de soleil, mais le temps
est frais dans l'ensemble. Il pleut
encore pas mal.*

*Il fait assez chaud, ou même
très chaud. Il fait sec; le soleil
brille. Les jours sont longs.*

Été

Automne

*Les feuilles tombent, les arbres
sont de toutes les couleurs,
c'est merveilleux. Il pleut souvent,
mais il ne fait pas vraiment froid.*

Hiver

*Il fait froid. Il pleut assez souvent.
Les jours sont courts. Parfois il neige,
mais la neige ne reste pas longtemps.
Il fait du vent.*

3. COMPARISONS BETWEEN THE UK LEARNER'S HOME TOWN AND A TOWN IN ANOTHER COUNTRY

- In lines 1, 3, 6, 8 and 9 which name should go in the gap - **your town** or **Bonn**?
- What will you put in the gaps in line 4?

Unterschiede zwischen | DEINER STADT | und **Bonn**

I. _____ ist viel kleiner als _____ .

II. Es gibt fast genau so viele Pubs. Falsch oder richtig? _____ .

III. Das Klima ist trockener in _____ .

IV. Durch beide Städte fließt ein Fluß.

   Bonn _____   Deine Stadt _____ .

V. Das kulturelle Angebot in _____ ist größer (viele Konzerte, Theater, Oper).

VI. In _____ gibt es viele Parks und Wälder.

VII. In _____ gibt es eine große Universität und 2 Fachhochschulen.

Différences entre LYON et | TA VILLE

- Put the name of **your town** and/or **Lyon**, in each of the gaps.

_____ est plus peuplé que _____ .

_____ est plus grand que _____ .

Il y a des musées à _____ .

Il y a des universités à _____ .

Il y a plusieurs centres commerciaux à _____ .

_____ est plus pollué que _____ .

Les gens sont plus chaleureux à _____ .

Il y a plusieurs gares à _____ .

Il y a un métro à _____ .

- Is the missing name an English place name or a German place name?
Say why you think so.

Was mache ich in [ ] *in meiner Freizeit?*

- *in Buchläden gehen*
- *Badminton spielen*
- *im Studentenchor mitsingen*
- *Fahrrad fahren*
- *Briefe schreiben*
- *durch Geschäfte gehen*
- *'Punch and Judy Shows' ansehen*
- *Straßenmusikanten zuhören*
- *Fernsehen gucken (Filme, Serien (aber nur 1 mal?)*
- *ins Theater gehen*
- *ins Kino gehen*

Einkaufsliste
für das Picknick

1 Schwarzbrot   250 g Frischkäse
2 Päckchen Butter   4 Brötchen

2 Stück Schwarzwälder Kirschtorte

100 g gekochter Schinken

100 g Schwarzwälder Schinken

100 g Aufschnitt   2 Stück Apfelstrudel

3 Tüten Chips

Obst (Bananen, Äpfel, Kiwis)

1 Dutzend Eier

5 Flaschen Sprudel   Schlagsahne
2 Flaschen Apfelsaft

D Comparison between shopping for a picnic in the UK and shopping for a picnic in another country

- Look at the German shopping list.
What could you not buy in a local English shop?
Go to your local supermarket and check.

5. COMPARISON BETWEEN SCHOOL IN THE UK AND SCHOOL IN ANOTHER COUNTRY

- List the differences and similarities between school in Germany and school in Britain.
  Which would you prefer? Why?

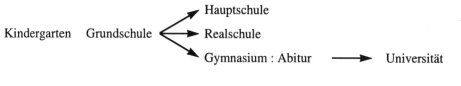

... Sonderschule

Kindergarten   Grundschule ⟶ Hauptschule
                              ⟶ Realschule
                              ⟶ Gymnasium : Abitur ⟶ Universität

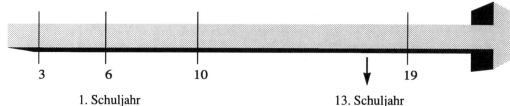

Alter

| 3 | 6 | 10 | | 19 |

1. Schuljahr   13. Schuljahr

Ein typischer Schultag

1.	7.30	-	8.15
2.	8.20	-	9.05
	9.05	-	9.20	'große Pause'
3.	9.25	-	10.10
4.	10.15	-	11.00
5.	11.05	-	11.50
6.	11.55	-	12.40

✓ keine Uniform
✓ keine 'Assembly'
✓ ab 14 Jahre kann man Religion abwählen
✓ Mittagessen zu Hause nach der Schule
✓ Klassenzimmer: die Lehrer wechseln den Raum
✓ Klassenbuch
✓ Noten von 1 ☺ bis 6 ☹
✓ wenn man in mehr als 2 Fächern 5 oder 6 steht, muß man das Jahr wiederholen (sitzenbleiben)
✓ statt Hauptschule, Realschule oder Gymnasium gehen manche Schüler in die Gesamtschule

6. COMPARISONS BETWEEN TRADITIONAL FESTIVALS

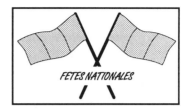

1er janvier	Fête du Nouvel An
6 janvier	Epiphanie
22 avril (Guadeloupe)	
27 mai (Martinique)	Fête de l'Abolition de l'esclavage
22 juin (Guyane)	
1er mai	Fête du travail
8 mai	Armistice de la guerre 1939-1945
14 juillet	Fête nationale
15 août	Assomption
1er novembre	La Toussaint
11 novembre	Armistice de la guerre 1914-1918
25 décembre	Noël

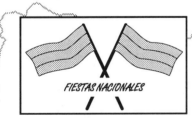

España es un país festivo por naturaleza.
Además de las fiestas locales o regionales tenemos algunas que se celebran en todo el país.
Algunas de ellas son:
- Día de los Reyes Magos (6 de enero): es el día de Navidad en el que recibimos los regalos
- 1ro de Mayo: día del trabajador
- Día del Pilar o Día de la Hispanidad (12 de octubre): celebramos el descubrimiento de América
- Día de la Constitución (6 de diciembre)
- Día de la Inmaculada (8 de diciembre)
- Día de Navidad

11

7. COMPARISONS BETWEEN ONE TRADITIONAL FESTIVAL IN ONE COUNTRY AND THAT OF THE UK

- Here is a local French Christmas tradition.
  Which of these 13 desserts have you eaten and which would you like to try?
  Do you have any foods which are a regional speciality?

Les 13 desserts – tradition provençale

- figues sèches
- abricots secs
- raisins
- bûche

- fougasse
- chocolats
- papillottes
- amandes
- noisettes

- dattes
- pruneaux
- mandarines
- noix

En général, on boit du champagne pour fêter la Nativité.

- Which of the items on this French Christmas shopping list would be on yours, too?

le sapin de noël
les boules
les guirlandes
une bougie
la crèche
un mouton miniature
un âne miniature
un petit Jésus
Marie
Joseph

du pain de mie
le saumon fumé
des citrons
une dinde
des marrons
des pommes de terre
la bûche de noël
les rois mages
un calendrier de Noël
le foie gras

des chocolats
du café
une bouteille de champagne
du Cognac
du Porto
une bouteille de vin blanc

- Which of the items on this German Christmas shopping list would be on yours, too?

Einkaufsliste für Heiligabend

- Tannenbaum
- Christbaumkugeln
- Lametta
  - Kerzen
  - Streichhölzer
  - Moos für die Krippe

- Königinpasteten (Blätterteigpasteten)
- 1 Dose Ragout Fin
- 1 Dose Pilze

- 10 Scheiben gekochten Schinken
- 1 Dose Spargel
- Mayonnaise

Spargelröllchen

- Weißbrot
- Butter
- 1 Fl. Wein   - Christstollen

13

- What does one French family have for Christmas dinner?
  Which of these foods or drink have you already eaten?
  What would you like to try?
  What do you eat at Christmas time and on which day: 24th
  December, 25th December ...?

Menu de Noël

- **Apéritif** :
  ****
  - jus de fruit
  - boissons alcoolisées
  - biscuits apéritifs, amuse-gueules
  - toasts au caviar, aux anchois, au fromage

- **Entrée** :
  *****
  - Coquilles Saint Jacques
  - boisson = vin blanc ou eau minérale

- **Repas principal** :
  - cuisses de dinde
  - légumes (pommes de terre rissolées,
    petits pois / carottes, haricots verts)
  - poisson pour les végétariens
  - sauce aux champignons
  - boisson = bière ou eau minérale

- **Plateau de fromages** :
  ****
  - pain, beurre
  - fromage de chèvre
  - boisson : vin rouge ou eau minéral.

- **Bûche de Noël** :
  ****
  - bûche pâtissière grand-marnier / vanille
  - champagne ou jus de fruit

- **Entremet** :
  ******
  - crème glacée
  - jus de fruit
  - tasse de café + verre de liqueur
  - chocolats, pralines, truffes

14

- List the foods which you have eaten and liked from this Italian description of dinner on 24th December.

Il Cenone di Natale

Questo è il menu :

antipasto
{
tartine al salmone
tartine al caviale
capitone

primi piatti
{
pennette al salmone
risotto di pesce

Secondi piatti
{
trota salmonata al forno
frittura di pesce

contorno
{
insalata
patate al forno
zucca, carciofi e cavoli fritti

formaggi vari

+
{
vino bianco e rosso
acqua
caffe
spumante

frutta
{
mandarini
mele
banane

dolci
{
panettone
pandoro
torrone biaco o al cioccolato

15

8. HELPING A FOREIGN VISITOR FEEL AT HOME

- Here is what two French people staying in England say they miss about France.
  Is there anything here you could do or buy in a shop near you to make up for what they miss about their home country?

Ce qui me manque...

la nourriture et surtout la viande rouge
la baguette de pain de la boulangerie qui
se trouve à côté de ma maison.

le saucisson sec
le beau temps
mon petit lapin
mes livres en Français
le Français
le bon café
le chocolat noir

- mes copains.
- ma famille.
- mon lit.
- ma chaîne-stéréo.
- le groupe de rock dans lequel je joue
- la bonne cuisine.
- les parties de cartes avec mes frères et sœurs

9. FESTIVALS AND CELEBRATIONS

- What does this French family celebrate?
  What do they do?

Chaque année, un mois après le Ramadan, les musulmans fêtent l'Aïd El Kebir ou la Tabaski. La journée commence très tôt par un petit déjeuner constitué de bouillie de miel et de lait. Ensuite, les hommes vont à la mosquée pour la prière du matin (vers 8h30 - 9h). A leur retour, chaque homme marié tue un bélier. Les femmes préparent beaucoup de grillades avec la viande, du couscous ou du riz avec beaucoup d'oignons et d'épices.
La veille, les femmes préparent des beignets et de la boisson constituée de jus d'oseille et de jus d'ananas mélangé ou du 'pin de singe' avec de la fleur d'oranger.
L'après-midi est consacré aux visites de famille et aux enfants qui reçoivent des pièces de monnaie des adultes. Tout le monde doit être habillé en tenue traditionnelle et, durant la soirée, il y a des boums.

AIM
To make comparisons between aspects of life in the UK and life in the target language country.

MATERIALS
A set of slides or colour photos which learners consider 'represent life in their home town' to be compared with a similar collection from the target language country.

SOURCE OF MATERIALS
Slides or colour photos are taken either by the UK learners themselves or by the teacher taking a group of learners in a minibus into their nearest town and asking them to say when a scene should be photographed. It is important that the **learners** indicate what should be photographed and also that they should know to whom the photos are to be sent.

One example of this task involved four Year 9 pupils, three girls and one boy. They were told that the photos were to be sent to 13 to 14-year old pupils in a secondary school in la Nouvelle Calédonie. They asked that the following photos should be taken. Their reasons, recorded in note form at the time, are quoted after each photo.

1	the Co-op mini supermarket
	'they should see one of our shops where we go shopping'
2	a woman pushing a pram
	'they probably carry babies on their backs over there'
3 & 4	a man posting a letter and a post box
	'they might not have letter boxes there'
5	the police station
	'so they can compare that with what their's looks like'
6	a fish and chip shop sign
	'so they can see what is typical English food'
7	an old white house covered in roses
	'that is a typical English house' (None of the pupils lived in a house like this but all felt it represented a typical English house more than their own.)
8	a pub with pupils sitting at a table outside
	'that's typical English'
9	a local stately home with one of the girls pointing it out
	'that's a famous house'
10	inside the local church with all five standing in pews pretending to sing hymns
	'because that's what you do in church' (The pupils admitted that none of them went to church regularly.)

11   inside the church a sixteenth century, Elizabethan marble effigy of a
       nobleman at prayer
       'that's a bit of English history'
12   a few neat rows of onions growing in one of their parent's allotments
       'that's where we grow our vegetables'
13   their school from the outside
       'that's our school' (Learners from Sawston Village College, Cambridge)

POSSIBLE TASKS
The possible task here is to send off the photos, requesting a collection of photos from
pupils in the other country. It is important that both groups of learners receive an
identical brief, namely to put together a collection of photos which they think
'represent life in their home town'.

EXAMPLE TASKS
Justifications or descriptions for what is sent off can be written (or recorded onto audio
cassette) in either English or the target language, depending on the ability of the group.
On the whole those teachers who have experimented with this project have found that it
is linguistically most beneficial if the pupils who **produce** the materials write in their
mother tongue. In this way those who **receive** the materials are given the foreign
language vocabulary necessary to talk about and refer to what they have received.
Many questions can be asked in this project about how representative or 'honest' the
image is that the learners are conveying.

Project 11   **Year 8/9 onwards**
Scattergrams

AIM
To make comparisons between aspects of life in the UK and life in the target language
country and to investigate language as an expression of culture.

MATERIALS
'Scattergrams' based on key concepts such as:

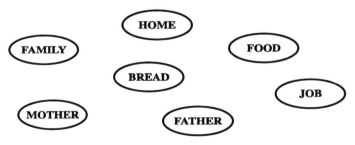

SOURCE OF MATERIALS

These can be obtained by asking groups of native speakers (FLAs, local people, exchange pupils on a visit to your school, pupils in a link school) to write on one sheet of papers all the things they think of when given one key concept, such as **food**. Each participant needs to be given white, unlined A4 paper and a black felt tip pen to allow clear photocopies to be made afterwards. Learners write their most spontaneous word associations nearest to the centre of the page, where the key concept is written. As their thoughts become slower and less spontaneous they put the words further away from the centre - written, obviously, in their target language equivalents.

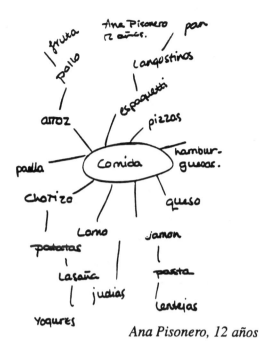

Ana Pisonero, 12 años

POSSIBLE TASKS

When these have been read, patterns of associations can be extracted and used not only for their content but for the language in which they are expressed. The foreign language learners can then write their own associated ideas (some key concepts in the target language and others in English) so that the receiving class can compare what they wrote originally with what the English foreign language learners have produced.

Project 12   **Year 8/9 onwards**
Stereotypes or is this *me*?

AIM
To investigate the validity of stereotypes.

MATERIALS
Responses to a questionnaire on 'what is it like to be English?'.

Here are two language versions of the questionnaire.

What is it like to be English?

My name is ....
I am ...... years old
I live in .... (town)
.... (country)

I think English people eat ....
I think English people drink ....
I think English people wear in summer ....
I think English people wear in winter ....
I think English people like ....
I think English people dislike ....
I think English people are good at ....
I think English people are bad at ....
I think English people are ....

Un Anglais, c'est qui?

Je m'appelle ....
J'ai .... ans
J'habite .... (ville / village)
en .... (pays)

Je pense que les Anglais
mangent ....
boivent ....
en été portent
(hommes) ....
(femmes) ....
en hiver portent
(hommes) ....
(femmes) ....
aiment ....
détestent ....
savent très bien ....
ne savent pas très bien ....
sont ....

Blank questionnaires are sent to a target language group for completion by 20+ respondents who are the same age as the group who will read and analyse the results.

POSSIBLE TASKS
Again when these questionnaires have been read, patterns of responses can be extracted and used not only for their content but for the language in which they are expressed. The foreign language learners can then write their own reactions to the questionnaire data, saying, in the target language or in English, whether they agree or disagree with it.

Project 13	Year 8 onwards
Contacts sans voyage	

AIM
To make comparisons between aspects of life in the UK and life in the target language country.

MATERIALS
Cassette, video, FAX, E-mail links, photographs, group dossiers.

SOURCE OF MATERIALS
Whole classes of learners in partner schools are linked person to person (or one to two if numbers do not match) and exchange once, twice or three times in a year some or all of: bilingual FAX, letters, audio cassettes, as well as target language cards, self portraits and photographs, news about themselves and their daily lives, special events, recipes, drawings, graphs and bar charts, menus, guide to and photographs of school, school timetables, postcards, tickets, labels, brochures, shop receipts, sporting programmes, newspapers etc.

POSSIBLE TASKS
Since the messages which are exchanged are bilingual, time can be spent in foreign language lessons preparing recordings and written work in the target language, as well as in English. There is a known (and named) audience for all communication and the purpose is quite explicitly to convey ideas and information to someone else and tell them something they do not know. This has a motivating force and for some learners may be the first time they have spoken or written to a real target language speaker!

(Further details are given in Barry Jones (ed), *Using authentic resources in teaching French* (CILT, 1984).

Gesture, facial expression and body language

AIM

To analyse what appears to identify one particular speech community.

MATERIALS AND SOURCE OF MATERIALS

Videos of (French/German/Spanish/Italian) speakers in their local context, as often seen in (French/German/Spanish/Italian) TV programmes which are made for a home audience or as language teaching materials.

POSSIBLE TASKS

Some well chosen extracts - and many extracts lend themselves to this treatment - can be played to a class without sound. It is the task for the class to analyse what they see, note and describe any gestures, facial expressions, or body language which they think is particular to the speech community. Visual and sound should then be played. These non-verbal features can then be transferred to a dramatised version of the original scene and the class can judge if the actors accurately represent what has been identified.

Who speaks it and where?

AIM

To demonstrate that the target language being taught is spoken throughout the world, either as a first language, or by the majority of a country's population or is a foreign language taught in a variety of countries.

MATERIALS

Travel brochures and written descriptions from French speakers who come from outside metropolitan France, or from other French speaking countries (from DOM / TOM countries, Belgium, Switzerland, Luxembourg, Canada etc) and written/printed descriptions which have been produced by learners of the target language in other countries (French written by Turkish learners in Ankara, Bulgarian learners etc). These examples can readily be extended to German, Spanish and Italian as these languages are spoken and learned by many people outside Germany, Spain and Italy.

Given a range of materials*, comparisons can be made between differing life styles of peoples who share the same language. In the case of material produced by other learners of the target language, this can be persuasive in demonstrating the usefulness of one particular target language as a lingua franca for many different peoples - an aspect not often experienced by foreign language learners in school.

Project 16	Year 7 onwards

Défense de ne pas toucher! Nicht berühren verboten!

AIM
To provide something tangible which can be physically examined by foreign language learners when appropriate topics occur in a foreign language learning programme.

MATERIALS
for a topic on 'food'
- food packets, wrappers, labels, pots, tins, price lists, posters, advertisements etc
- recipe + real ingredients to make and eat, for example,
  croque-monsieur, salade de tomates, sandwich au saucisson sec, sandwich au fromage, tarte aux pommes, etc;

for a topic on 'school'
stationery goods in priced packets (unopened!) to get ready for *la rentrée*;

for a topic on 'first aid'
bandages, safety pins, plasters, scissors, aspirin, antiseptic cream etc (This serves both for classroom demonstration of First Aid techniques and for classroom emergencies!).

All of the above can be collected from a trip abroad either by members of the teaching staff or by groups of children on an exchange visit or as a result of a request to a person in the country.

POSSIBLE TASKS
There are a number of tasks, some of which are implied in the above. Food containers can be compared with UK equivalents, if such exist, and examined for contents, price, ingredients, as well as being simply objects which can be associated with words to aid memorisation and referencing for the learner. Some foods can be made and tasted with ratings given.

---

*   see contact addresses on p36.

Stationery goods can be priced and prices compared with those in the UK. Costing *la rentrée* in France can be an interesting exercise, especially if compared with a UK equivalent. At another level, advertising for *la rentrée* in France can be compared with 'back to school' in the UK. Differences and similarities in attitude and practice can be investigated and documented.

Project 17   **Year 8/9 onwards**
What the media says

AIM
To collect expressions of opinion about target language speakers from the media.

MATERIALS
English newspapers, other language newspapers, magazines, TV programmes in UK and elsewhere.

POSSIBLE TASKS
To collect statements made in the media about other peoples, and assess the validity of the statements made, where possible, in the light of evidence rather than prejudice. This project is one which lends itself to display, provided that each piece of evidence is accompanied by a balanced, evaluative statement produced by the foreign language learners.

Project 18   **Year 8 onwards**
Class-to-class FAX

AIM
To communicate on a regular basis with a class of pupils about everyday interests, concerns and information. These can include cross-curricular themes, such as weather changes, environmental issues, local town /village surveys, patterns of consumerism, or be more simply an exchange of personal information about family, pets, school timetables, leisure activities, 'how I spend a Saturday/Sunday' etc.

SOURCE OF MATERIALS
FAX, E-mail links.

If electronic communication is possible, even occasionally, then the motivation gained from the immediacy of sending a message and receiving a reply is considerable. FAX is relatively inexpensive and has the advantage that learners can transmit images, such as drawings, maps, charts, as well as text. An agreement should be reached that all sheets are A4 with good margins, and text and drawings etc should be in black. Legibility (and photocopiability) will then be ensured.

Project 19	Year 7 onwards
Whole class surveys	

AIM
To make comparisons between aspects of life in the UK and life in the target language country.

MATERIALS
Surveys and questionnaire responses **especially from a whole class** in the target language country, e.g.:

- which sports are played and/or watched by members of the class;
- which are the class's most popular leisure activities;
- which jobs do the class have to do at home;
- how much pocket money is received and what do the members of the class spend it on
- what is a typical breakfast;
- how many members of the class go to church, the synagogue, the mosque, etc, weekly / in December;
- which magazines are the most popular amongst members of one class (send a copy of the top three!);
- which kinds of television programme do members of the class watch most (send a copy of the radio / TV programme guide).

SOURCE OF MATERIALS
The survey results may be collected by asking a FLA who may well have contact with English teachers in his or her home country, and/or by asking other native speakers (e.g. in exchange school, partner school, linked class, family) at home or abroad. E-mail links are particularly appropriate here.

POSSIBLE TASKS
Compare evidence from the target language country with similar evidence from the UK class. Emphasis, as in all comparisons, is put on positive opinion and what is attractive, rather than what is considered negatively strange or unattractive.

AIM

To provide a **sustained, enjoyable and successful experience** of listening to and responding in the target language and to engage in as many pursuits as possible normally reserved for the target language community.

MATERIALS

For a foreign language day games, outside and indoor, can be played. A French day can include outdoor games such as boules, handball, and indoor games such as a French version of Monopoly, *le Jeu des 7 Familles*, *Mille Bornes*, and other card games if appropriate. Other non one-country specific possibilities are:
- a range of ball games;
- making another country's food from a recipe: to be eaten at midday;
- a Treasure Hunt / Hunt the Criminal using clues /Alibi;
- learning a regional dance;
- an element from another subject to be taught in the target language (Geography, Home Economics, PE, Maths, History all have topics which can be taught without huge resource demands in the target language);
- making up a newspaper or TV programme to be video'd during the day with editor, journalists, actors, presenter and sources of information, some of which could be on-line (Minitel via Campus 2000). Advertisements and jingles for goods from the target country are always popular;
- presenting famous people from the target country; match name to profession or occupation;
- putting captions to cartoons, works of art (paintings by the Belgian painter, Magritte, cartoons by Sempé etc are very suitable for this activity);
- sorting images into their country of origin (France, Germany, Spain, Italy, Netherlands etc) using the target language names for each country and a collection of images collected by members of a class prior to the day.

4   Cultural awareness project: Council of Europe

Year 8/9

This is a project which was launched at the Council of Europe's Workshop 13A in Genoa in December 1993. The report which follows outlines the pilot study carried out from January to July 1994. Of those responsible for co-ordinating work with schools in their own country one is making bilingual German - English contacts, one bilingual French - English, one bilingual Spanish - English, two are communicating in French as their lingua franca, and three are communicating entirely in English.

AIM
The aim of the pilot project is to see how each country's 13 to 14-year old school pupils portray their own nationality to children of the same age in another country. The project believes that one country's foreign language learners will only begin to understand the way of life of another country if they begin to look first at their own.

MATERIALS AND SOURCE OF MATERIALS
To do this in a practical way the project asked for schools in Britain to:
1 find a group of willing 13 to 14-year old pupils;
2 ask them to fill a real shoebox (or similar size) with objects which **they believe** represent their country and the English way of life.

They were encouraged to discuss as a group:

• **what** should go in the box;
• **why** each object is chosen.

Each pupil also wrote, in brief, his or her reasons, in the target language or mother tongue, for including each object in the box.

When filled the box was sent to a secondary school in one of the 32 European Union countries. Later a box was sent back to the UK school.

The initial letter sent out to children in one UK school is included below since it illustrates the detail of the project (see Appendix 1, p37).

27

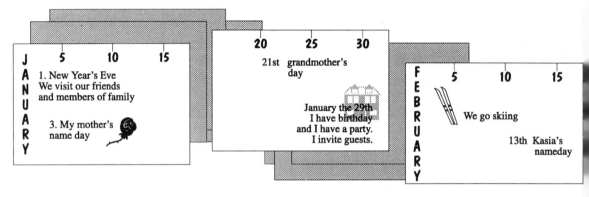

Since its beginning in December, 1993, the project has aroused interest not only within the group of original participants but with an increasingly wide range of other people. The idea of secondary school foreign language learners filling a shoebox with objects, papers, wrappers, tickets and numerous other items which they believe represent their way of life has proved appealing. For the recipients there has been an increasing understanding of how others live, as well as a certain questioning of how the objects they choose to send portray their own culture and way of life. As boxes are exchanged and the contents are analysed questions inevitably arise. Children want to ask why some of the contents were included, why some were omitted, what some mean, how representative some 'pieces of evidence' are. These are all questions which are sent back to be answered by pupils in the other country, and, significantly, their answers often provoke further questions. Understandings become refined, generalisations are modified. The complexity of a person's cultural identity begins to emerge.

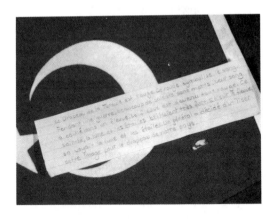

EXCHANGE OF MATERIALS

The language of explanation has been target language + English. In an Ankara - Cambridge exchange pupils in both schools communicated with each other in French, their only common language of communication. This feature really emphasises an aspect of foreign language learning not often experienced by learners, namely the use of the target language as the **only** language possible if communication is to take place. In a Getafe - Cambridge exchange the Spanish and English children used a principled mix of English and Spanish.

Other materials and information that have been sent to Cambridgeshire schools include:

- A '**dateline**', or sort of calendar of events on which pupils list all the important personal, school, national, international events of the year, explained through writing, drawings, pictures (a description kindly provided by Mary Rose Mifsud,

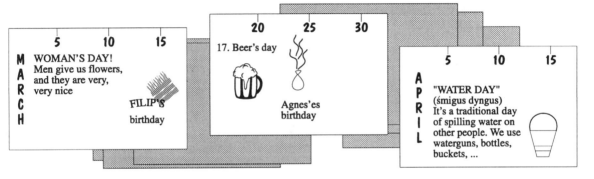

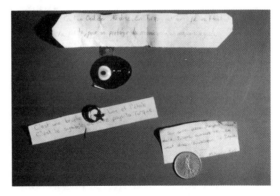

Valletta, Malta). A 'dateline' received from Warsaw (illustrated, in parts, on pp28-33), was beautifully presented. It was eight metres long, consisted of 24 sheets of paper joined together lengthways and was the work, done in English, of all members of one class of pupils.

- A questionnaire *What is it like to be English?*, (French version from Belgium, Turkey and Bulgaria).

RECORD KEEPING AND DOCUMENTATION OF THE PROJECT

In order to keep a record of the way the project developed and was being used by pupils in all the participating schools, every item included in the shoeboxes exchanged during the pilot phase was logged. Since this now seems to give a fairly representative view of the *kinds* of contents which pupils put in shoeboxes, a decision was made to limit logging of contents to items which were a *new development*, or were sent *in response to documented pupils' questions and requests*. Such a record, including questions on the item illustrated and appropriate answers from the partner school, will then document the evolution of pupils' understandings of other cultures and ways of life *over time*, an important theme emerging from the initial exchange of boxes.

Other records kept are:

- all questionnaire responses referred to earlier.

- a second questionnaire (see Appendix 2, p38) given to English children when they receive a shoebox. This questionnaire attempts to describe the pupils' perceptions of other teenagers in different countries based on the shoebox contents. So far children in Cambridgeshire schools have characterised their views of what it is like to be Turkish in Ankara and Spanish in Gatafe. The use of this second questionnaire was

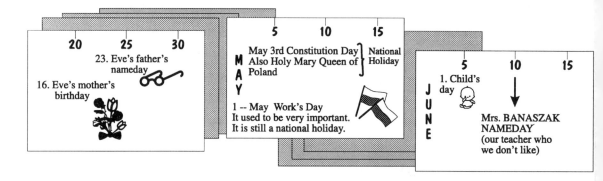

not introduced until it was realised that no permanent record was being kept of pupils' initial understandings of 'otherness' and how this understanding changed over time as the exchange of materials continued. Although the example given is in English because the Year 7 group involved was not linguistically very advanced, more able groups can attempt answers in the foreign language. It is, of course, not possible to devise a questionnaire such as this until the contents of the shoebox are revealed. The example shows the collaborative effort of a geographer and a foreign language teacher.

- written descriptions of reasons given by pupils for including each item in the shoebox. This is vital evidence in trying to establish how children see themselves and their culture when they are conveying this to their peers in other countries.

- written accounts by teachers and others describing how they were adopting or adapting the shoebox project for use with their own classes. This has taken the form, to date, of written descriptions and evaluations of the project, notes on its implementation in class or an extensive report. (For an example of this see Appendix 3, p39.)

WAYS OF WORKING

For schools who exchange shoeboxes the project suggests that, **before sending a shoebox** a teacher can:

(the example which follows comes from Hanna Kijowska in Warsaw, Poland)

Step 1   Discuss with a class what differences and similarities there might be between living in their country and living in the shoebox sender's country. Teachers are asked to keep notes of this discussion.

Step 2   Ask pupils to bring to school something that they feel represents their family. As Hanna Kijowska commented, 'At first the children think nothing of this request. But the following day they arrive with comments on how difficult it is to find something or to decide on one object. In the end three people finally decide to bring something which describes themselves.' Teachers are asked to keep lists of what the pupils bring.

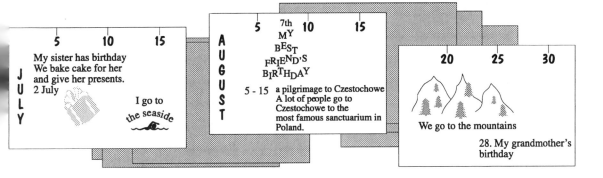

In the example from Warsaw the list included, *before* some items were discarded -

- a book of poems by national poet, Adam Mickiewicz;
- a biography of Chopin;
- a book of music;
- a collection of coins;
- a collection of stamps;
- a little black cat, ceramics;
- a couple of dolls in Greek national costume;
- a car map of Poland and a sea shell;
- a plant;
- a book on flowers and animals;
- pictures from the races, horses;
- a detective story;
- crosswords - one homemade;
- a book of comics Astérix, Bhagavadgita;
- a newspaper;
- a painting.

Step 3   Put all the objects into a box (without the other pupils knowing who has brought what), and present the objects, one by one, to the class. Groups of four pupils can then discuss each item, try to guess who brought it and write comments. Some objects are very easy to identify, others obviously not. The following day each pupil can pick out an object brought in by somebody else and try to guess or explain why it has been chosen to represent a family. Immediately afterwards the owner gives his or her explanation. Pupils can then write an evaluation of the activity which can be kept by their teacher.

Step 4   Lastly, open the shoebox (received from England in the example from Poland) and work as described in Step 3, namely in groups who study the shoebox contents, discuss them and write down their feelings and first reactions. They can also be encouraged to write down their questions to send to the partner school, in this case in England. A record of the questions should be kept for reference purposes later.

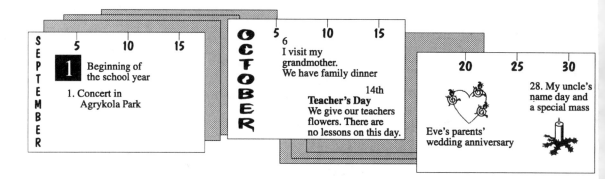

Step 5   Ask the class to write a letter (to England) and create a (Polish) shoebox in response to their own discussions in Step 3 and in Step 4. Teachers are asked to photocopy any such letter and list the contents of the shoebox, together with the pupil's reasons for including them.

When sending a box, every teacher:

1   asks each pupil to write what he/she has put in the shoebox and the reason for the item's inclusion on a piece of paper attached to it;

2   lists the total contents of the box and the first name of the pupil who is responsible for each item;

and, **before receiving a box**, every teacher:

asks every pupil in the class to write on a piece of paper their name, age, and what they know and what they think of the way of life of pupils in the sending country **before** they open the box. This they can do in their own language, if appropriate. (If the sending school is an English school (not Irish, Scottish or Welsh) please use the questionnaire provided on p20.)

and, **after opening a box**, every teacher:

1   asks every pupil in the class to complete the questionnaire provided on page 38 or an adapted form of it. This has already been shown to provide insights into how children interpret the evidence contained in the shoebox;

2   writes notes or an account of how they dealt with the shoebox in addition to 1 and 2 above;

3   asks every pupil to fill in a French or English version of the questionnaire shown on p20. Participating teachers are asked not to change the wording of this.

32

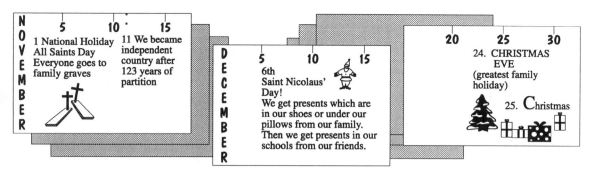

Elements of the project, from the experience of the pilot phase January - July 1994, which need improvement.

The following comments come from various participants:

Problem 1
'Maltese students were exposed to an English opinion of themselves. But the shoebox was misleading at times; for example in the box which arrived from the UK there was neither a teabag nor any reference to royalty. So Maltese students concluded that these may not be as important as they're said to be for English people. In another box sent by an English class, of which our co-ordinator sent us photocopies of the contents, both items featured prominently. It would seem therefore that the strategy may be too limiting and limited at times.'

Comment
Since there is no limit to the number of boxes to be sent from one country to another, nor is there any restriction on what is to be included it is suggested that the Maltese children ask their English counterparts why they chose not to include these or any other items. In this way the English children may be made more aware of the image that their shoebox is creating, and may (or may not!) wish to correct it. A two-way conversation can be started with some interesting questions; such a conversation could be written or recorded on audio-cassette if appropriate.

Problem 2
'A problem of logistics concerned the postal contact between us and our European counterparts... Thus the envisaged contact, comparison and cross-fertilization of ideas was delayed.'

Comment
In the first two months of the project there was an inevitable delay caused by the necessity to contact and brief local schools and teachers who knew nothing of the project. In their turn, they had then to integrate the discussion and collection of shoebox materials into their work schemes. One school (Linton Village College, Cambridge) took ten schooldays to do this, another (St Ivo School, St Ives,

Cambridgeshire) eleven weeks and quite justifiably so, given the extent of the project which they developed in French and PSE timetabled slots. Once, however, each school has launched its own link the time to be taken can be negotiated with the partner school. This will avoid disappointment for the participating learners.

Another way to avoid long delays when nothing is received is to send some of the materials at regular intervals. A 'dateline' can be sent first, then an audiocassette and/or FAX a week later, then a shoebox. Similarly, when a new group of schools is involved, both can agree to send the first box at the same time, on an agreed date. The exchange of questions and related materials can then follow as and when the partner schools can manage the exchange. Books, songs, postcards, photos, newspapers etc can also be sent in response to questions asked by children in one or other school at regular intervals.

Elements of the project, from the experience of the pilot phase January - July 1994, which have worked well.

This section of the report can best perhaps be served by a verbatim quotation from an evaluation carried out by Mary Rose Mifsud at the end of May 1994.

Objectives

To see whether a deliberate input of culture would help students:
a. learn English better (language awareness)
b. engage in self-awareness
c. understand English culture
d. become more tolerant of other people's values, beliefs and life-styles.

Results

Students:
a. enjoyed the project and practised a number of social and cognitive skills, including: prioritising, categorising, selecting, debating, consensus-building, inferring and forming opinions from evidence. There was a marked increase in students' oracy.
b. were made aware of their own culture through research, reading and discussion. They also learnt English vocabulary connected with Maltese cultural events. This linguistic area is usually problematic.
c. were exposed to English culture through the use of video, realia as well as standard written material.
d. were exposed to the English opinion of themselves.
e. learnt more about the culture than if the component had been left to chance.

Such an evaluation gives an optimistic view of the value of the project.

Conclusion

Whether small scale or large scale the importance of developing an awareness of and respect for others is without question. It is hoped that this book will add to most teachers' already extensive repertoire of activities which give their learners access to the lives, concerns and environments of people living in this and other countries. As a summary of what has been proposed, the following would seem to be key ideas and processes:

START WITH THE LEARNERS
- how do we see ourselves?   e.g.:   what would you choose as being 'your world' to show a visitor?
  This demonstrates a 'best side' approach, gives an idea of the things that learners believe interests others and begins to raise awareness about the nature of evidence.

- how do we see others?   e.g.:   what do you think the (French) are like?
  This can show dominant features of a currently held stereotype. It can be turned into an hypothesis rather than a fact and can lead to a request for evidence.

DECIDE WHAT CONSTITUTES RELIABLE EVIDENCE
- set up an IMAGES board

PROVISIONAL	PERMANENT

- collect statements from the press, books, adults, peers, FLA
- ask: - what do you make of this evidence?
  - do you want to shift any statement from either column after one week, one month, two months...?
  - do you still believe what you said one week, one month, two months... ago?
  - what made you change your mind?
  - what do you believe now?

TEST HYPOTHESES
- use primary sources:
  - scattergrams, bar charts, pie-charts from partner school/class
  - interviews
  - printed materials
  - posters
  - letters
  - native speakers at home and abroad
  - the media;
- use secondary sources: books, reference materials, coursebooks;
- use on-line resources (e.g. Minitel) if available;
- make comparisons;
- evaluate what you have explored.

Related reading

Alix C and G Bertrand (eds), 'Pour une pédagogie des échanges' in *Le Français dans le Monde*: numéro spécial février-mars (Edicef, 1994)

Mares C (ed), *Our Europe: environmental awareness and language development through school exchanges: The keep Britain tidy schools research project* (Brighton Polytechnic, 1985)

Useful addresses

The Schools' Unit, Central Bureau, Seymour Mews House, Seymour Mews, London W1H 9PE
for contact with other classes in France, Germany, Austria, Belgium, Italy, Spain etc

Service culturel, Ambassade de France, 23 Cromwell Road, London, SW7
for contact with countries and schools which teach French as a foreign language

Goethe-Institut, 50 Princes Gate, Exhibition Road, London, SW7 2PH
for contact with countries and schools which teach German as a foreign language

Istituto Italiano, 39 Belgrave Square, London, SW1X 8NX
for contact with countries and schools which teach Italian as a foreign language

Embajada de España, 20 Peel Street, London, W8 7PD
for contact with countries and schools which teach Spanish as a foreign language

National Council for Educational Technology, Milburn Hill Road, Science Park, Coventry CCV4 7JJ
for information on the use of E-mail and all forms of IT

Appendix 1

CAN YOU HELP PLEASE ?

A secondary school in Malta is asking a secondary school in some of the 32 European countries to send a shoebox (or similar sized container) containing objects or papers which people your age say represent life in their country. **Your** school is the only English school participating so we are relying on you!

So can you, please, this weekend, collect objects, papers etc which, in your opinion, are clues to help the Maltese school discover what it is to be English. Please do not buy anything and don't forget they must all fit into a shoebox!

Here are some ideas of what to consider:

- labels
- postcards
- photos - houses, rooms in houses, gardens etc
- lists of what you eat at each meal in a day
- school booklets, rules, ...
- wrappers - for food, drinks with or without photos
- publicity papers
- adverts
- tickets
- cuttings from Radio Times or TV Times
- newspaper cuttings and/or photos
- lists of favourite sports, games, pets, foods
- drawings of places, people
- **small** empty boxes or containers

    + anything you can think of...!

Please give anything you decide to include in the box

to .... in Room .... on ....

Thank you very much if you can help.

Appendix 2

Example of a questionnaire devised by a modern language teacher and a geographer to encourage learners to evaluate the contents of a shoebox.

H O M E R T O N   C O L L E G E ,   C A M B R I D G E

NAME _____   AGE _____
CLASS _____   SCHOOL _____

THE SHOEBOX FROM TURKEY

Look at what is in the box and say what you have found out about Turkey. Describe the object or objects which gave you this idea.

_____

Can you say something about:

> its climate
>
> its politics
>
> its customs
>
> its buildings
>
> its leisure pursuits
>
> its food
>
> its clothes
>
> anything else

Did anything surprise you? If so, what? _____
Did anything not surprise you? If so, what? _____

What image do you have now of the country and the people?

_____

Do you want to ask any questions about any of the contents in the Turkish shoebox? Say which object and what your question is:
OBJECT _____   QUESTION _____

Based on what you have seen in the shoebox what do you want to send back that shows what it is like to be English? Say why! _____

Appendix 3

Extract from a report by Mᵃ Luisa García Torralba, I.E.S. Getafe X, Getafe, Spain.

SELECTION OF MATERIAL

When we told the students about a cultural interchange with another country, they felt really interested in the matter.

We encouraged them to bring 'things' to the classroom which could be interesting for foreign people trying to understand our culture. Those things chosen should be small enough to be kept in a shoebox.

The next step, once the material was collected in the classroom, was to explain on a piece of paper the reasons why they had chosen those objects. Though they worked in groups of two, three and even four people, they were sometimes helped by their teachers.

The list of material selected in our shoebox is shown below:

El Palacio Real	Football pools
the aquaduct of Segovia	a fan
a tape (*sevillanas*)	a badge of the 'Real Madrid football team'
la cibeles	the hymn of the 'Real Madrid football team'
the Prado Museum	the Spanish flag
bus, train and underground tickets	Madrid underground map
a photograph of the students	parque de '*el retiro*'
the Spanish omelette recipe	

ACTIVITIES USING THE MATERIAL RECEIVED FROM THE OTHER COUNTRY DESIGNED TO:

- make a comparison between the objects received and those which have been sent;
- get a knowledge of the Spanish image from the point of view of non Spanish people;
- make students guess, without a previous explanation, the purpose of the material received;
- make a comparison of the different objects with those for the same purpose in our country; differences in size, colour, shape, material they are made of etc;
- make students take part in debates, discussions, in which they will be able to understand the way of thinking etc of other countries.

José Angel Gil (3° B)	tuna tin label
Julián Cano (1° Bach)	football pool
	'*La Quiniela*'
José Antonio Hidalgo (1° Bach)	fun park: postcard
Javier Domingo (1° Bach)	magazine cutting from the '*Puta Mili*'
Mónica Nieto (1° Bach)	a drawing of Olympic Games mascot
Cristina Ruiz (3° C)	a tiny bull
Juan Manuel Aguilar (3° C)	a postcard: *La Manga*
Ricardo Crespo (1° Bach)	a pin of Real Madrid, a football team
Manoli Chica (1° Bach)	*Las Castañuelas*
Macarena Rodríguez (1° Bach)	ticket from Expo '92
Beatriz Prieto (1° Bach)	a picture from *Feria de Abril*
Gema Jiménez (1° Bach)	'*Polvorón*' wrapper
Samuel Esteban (3° C)	a leaflet of San Isidro Festivals and some recipes
Raquel Recas (3° C)	Spanish omelette recipe
Ann Belén Álvarez (1° Bach)	Spanish omelette recipe
Amparo Blanco (1° Bach)	Paella recipe
Antonio Piñas (1° Bach)	three different pesetas
Ronda y Ana Belén (3° B)	a little bull and a leather wine bottle
Sonia Triviño (3° B)	COBI
Jaime Gª Recuero	*Banderín de Toledo*
David Nicolás (1° A)	Spanish stew: *COCIDO MADRILEÑO*
David Marcos (3° C)	a postcard: Avila
Javier Gª Culpián (3° C)	a photograph
Rafael Rosa (3° C)	a flag
Sonia Miñaca (3° C)	*plano del Metro*
Daniel Ricardo Romero (3° B)	timetable

A shoebox from England to War
contained the follow

Russell	newspaper cuttings from the Cambridge Evening News
Tom	community programmes of events
Adam	letter to parents (from school)
Jonathan	football programme
Jamie	rail map for Network South East
Eleanor	herbal tea bag (full!)
Jemma	label from baked beans tin
Tessa	Sainsbury's till receipt, Christmas card
Helen T.	Tower of London guide, postcards of London
Christiana	book of nursery rhymes, English coins
Hannah	Yorkshire tea packet, vinegar label
Jenny	pages from TV Times, own drawings of school uniform
Cheryl	local newspaper cuttings
Hayley	bus tickets, photos of famous people
Claire	'Take That' photo, school lesson timetable, badge from Wimpey
Hayley	badges, leisure Centre programme
Jenny	teenage magazines
Susannah	Royal Wedding souvenir booklet: 'getting rid of the evidence!'
Michael	school newsletter to parents
Russell	Lord's cricket score card
Helen M.	Royal photos cut from a national newspaper
Emma	packet of Choc-n-Toffee (full!), Cup-a-soup packet, also full